Golf is like a love affair.
If you don't take it seriously,
it's no fun; if you do take it seriously,
it breaks your heart.

Arnold Daly

This edition © Robert Frederick Ltd. 1996 Old Orchard Street, Bath BA1 1JU
First published 1996; All rights reserved.
Printed and bound in China

THE GOLFER'S
BOOK OF QUOTATIONS

Golf is a typical capitalist
lunacy of upper-class
Edwardian England.

George Bernard Shaw

The Golfer's Book of Quotations

Golf is a good walk spoiled.

Mark Twain

❦

Golf is a game in which a ball – one and a half inches in diameter –
is placed on a ball – 8,000 miles in diameter.
The object being to hit the small ball, but not the larger.

John Cunningham

❦

Only religious ceremonies proceed with more respect than
the major golf tournaments in this country.

Jimmy Cannon

The Golfer's Book of Quotations

There is one essential only in the golf swing, the ball must be hit.

Sir Walter Simpson

❧

He's hit it fat. . . . It will probably be short. . . . It just hit the front edge of the green. . . . It's got no chance. . . . It's rolling but it will stop. . . . It's rolling toward the cup. . . . Well, I'll be damned!

Jimmy Demaret (commentating at the World Championship in 1953 on Lew Worsham's winning wedge shot)

❧

All I have against it is that it takes you so far from the clubhouse

Eric Linklater

The Golfer's Book of Quotations

At my first Masters, I got the feeling that if I didn't play well,
I wouldn't go to heaven.

Dave Marr

A golf course is the epitome of all that is purely transitory in the universe,
a space not to dwell in, but to get over as quickly as possible.

Jean Giraudoux

I never pray on the golf course. Actually, the Lord answers
my prayers everywhere except on the course.

Billy Graham

The Golfer's Book of Quotations

Golf is a fickle game, and must be wooed to be won.

Willy Park Jr

My game is so bad I gotta hire three caddies – one to walk the left rough,
one for the right rough, and one down the middle.
And the one in the middle doesn't have much to do.

Dave Hill

Golf is not like tennis, or basketball, or football,
where you can control your opponent.
With golf you cannot control your opponent.

Tom Kite

The Golfer's Book of Quotations

I don't like doctors. They are like golfers.
Every one has a different answer to your problem.

Severiano Ballesteros

When Nicklaus plays well he wins, when he plays badly he comes second.
When he's playing terribly, he's third.

Johnny Miller

Golf is deceptively simple, endlessly complicated. A child can play it well
and a grown man can never master it.
It is almost a science, yet a puzzle with no answer.

Arnold Palmer

The Golfer's Book of Quotations

I have found, in my own matches, that if you just keep throwing consistent, unvarying bogeys and double bogeys at your opponents, they will crack up sooner or later from the pressure.

Rex Lardner

❧

It's funny, but the more I practice, the luckier I become.

Gary Player

❧

One reason golf is such an exasperating game is that a thing learned is so easily forgotten and we find ourselves struggling year after year with faults we had discovered and corrected time and time again.

Robert T. 'Bobby' Jones

The Golfer's Book of Quotations

My goal this year is basically to find the fairways.

Lauri Peterson

❧❦❧

My golf swing is like ironing a shirt.
You get one side smoothed out, turn it over and there is a big wrinkle on the other side. You iron that side, turn it over and there's another wrinkle.

Tom Watson

❧❦❧

The vital thing about a hole is that it should either be more difficult than it looks or look more difficult than it is.
It must never be what it looks.

Sir Walter Simpson

The Golfer's Book of Quotations

All games are silly, but golf, if you look at it dispassionately, goes to extremes.

Peter Alliss

❧

Anytime you get the urge to golf, instead take 18 minutes and beat your head against a good solid wall! This is guaranteed to duplicate to a tee the physical and emotional beating you would have suffered playing a round of golf. If 18 minutes aren't enough, go for 27 or 36 – whatever feels right.

Mark Oman

❧

What's over there? A nudist colony?

Lee Trevino (after his 3 playing partners drove into the woods)

PHILOSOPHER (*eight down to bogey*). "Anyway I don't suppose for one moment the cup is real silver."

You hit the ball and if it doesn't go far enough you just hit it again, and if that doesn't work, you hit it again, and so on.

Robert Robinson

The Golfer's Book of Quotations

I still swing the way I used to, but when I look up the ball
is going in a different direction.

Lee Trevino

❦

There are now more golf clubs in the world than Gideon Bibles,
more golf balls than missionaries and, if every golfer in the world,
male and female, were laid end to end, I for one would leave them there.

Michael Parkinson

❦

The difference between learning to play golf and learning to drive
a car is that in golf you never hit anything.

Anon

The Golfer's Book of Quotations

Golf appeals to the idiot in us and the child . . . Just how childlike golf players become is proven by their frequent inability to count past five.

John Updike

❧

As of this writing, there are approximately 2,450 reasons why a person hits a rotten shot, and more are being discovered every day.

Jay Cronley

❧

There's only one thing wrong about Babe and me. I hit like a girl and she hits like a man.

Bob Hope (referring to Babe Didrikson Zaharias)

The Golfer's Book of Quotations

When ground rules permit a golfer to improve his lie, he can either move his ball or change the story about his score.

Anon

Actually, the only time I ever took out a one-iron was to kill a tarantula. And I took a seven to do that.

Jim Murray

Anytime a golfer hits a ball perfectly straight with a big club it is, in my view, a fluke.

Jack Nicklaus

The Golfer's Book of Quotations

The right way to play golf is to go up and hit the bloody thing.

George Duncan

❧

The entire handbook can be reduced to three rules. One: you do not touch
your ball from the time you tee it up to the moment you pick it out of the hole.
Two: don't bend over when you are in the rough. Three: when you are in the
woods, keep clapping your hands.

Charles Price

❧

Suffering – ! I've got a hen back home in Charlotte
that can lay an egg further than that!

Clayton Heafner, (missing a 3 inch putt to lose the Oakland Open by one shot)

If you watch a game, it's fun.
If you play it, it's recreation.
If you work at it, it's golf.

Bob Hope

The Golfer's Book of Quotations

I'd like to see the fairways more narrow.
Then everybody would have to play from the rough, not just me.

Severiano Ballesteros

❦

I visualise hitting the ball as far as JoAnne Carner, putting like Amy Alcott,
looking like Jan Stephenson and having Carol Mann's husband.

Dinah Shore

❦

You've got to turn yourself into a material as soft as putty,
and then just sort of slop the clubhead through.
You'll hit much farther and with less effort.

Johnny Miller

The Golfer's Book of Quotations

Caddies are a breed of their own. If you shoot a 66, they'll say, 'Man, we shot a 66!' But go and shoot 77 and they'll say, 'Hell, he shot a 77!'

Lee Trevino

If ah didn't have these ah'd hit it twenty yards further.

Babe Didrikson Zaharias (referring to her breasts)

Thou shalt not use profanity; thou shalt not covet thy neighbour's putter; thou shalt not steal thy neighbour's ball; thou shalt not bear false witness in the final tally.

Ground Rules: Clergyman's Golf Tournament, Grand Rapids

The Golfer's Book of Quotations

He quit playing when I started outdriving him.

JoAnne Carner (referring to her husband Don)

❦

Everybody has two swings – a beautiful practice swing and a choked-up one with which they hit the ball. So it wouldn't do either of us a damned bit of good to look at your practice swing.

Ed Furgol

❦

I don't think that was me that shot that eighty-four. It must have been somebody else. Actually, I was trying to get my handicap squared away.

Fuzzy Zoeller

The Golfer's Book of Quotations

Real golfers tape The Masters so they can go play themselves.

George W Roope

❦

Through years of experience I have found that air offers
less resistance than dirt.

Jack Nicklaus explaining why he tees up the ball so high

❦

I remember being upset once and telling my Dad I wasn't following
through right, and he replied,
'Nancy, it doesn't make any difference to a ball what you do after you hit it.'

Nancy Lopez

The Golfer's Book of Quotations

Ah well. If we hit it perfect every day, everybody else would quit.

Lee Trevino to Tom Watson

❦

When he gets the ball into a tough place, that's when he's most relaxed.
I think it's because he has so much experience at it.

Don Christopher (Jack Lemon's caddie)

❦

Well, in plain old English, I'm driving it bad, chipping bad, putting bad,
and not scoring at all. Other than that, and the fact I got up this morning,
I guess everything's okay.

Bob Wynn

The Golfer's Book of Quotations

Golf is a game in which you yell Fore, shoot six, and write down five.

Paul Harvey

❧❧❧

When a putter is waiting his turn to hole-out a putt of one or two feet in length, on which the match hangs at the last hole, it is of vital importance that he think of nothing.
At this supreme moment he ought studiously to fill his mind with vacancy. He must not even allow himself the consolation of religion.

Sir Walter Simpson

❧❧❧

Keep on hitting it straight until the wee ball goes in the hall.

James Braid

The Golfer's Book of Quotations

I only hit the ball about 220 off the tee, but I can always find it.

Bonnie Lauer

❧❧❧

Golf increases the blood pressure, ruins the disposition, spoils the digestion, induces neurasthenia, hurts the eyes, callouses the hands, ties kinks in the nervous system, debauches the morals, drives men to drink or homicide, breaks up the family, turns the ductless glands into internal warts, corrodes the pneumo-gastric nerve, breaks off the edges of the vertebrae, induces spinal meningitis and progressive mendacity, and starts angina pectoris.

Dr. A S Lamb

❧❧❧

My Handicap?: Woods and irons.

Chris Codiroli

The Golfer's Book of Quotations

My caddie had the best answer to that —
'Just to let the other one know it can be replaced.'
Larry Nelson explaining why he carried two putters

❧

Never give up. If we give up in this game, we'll give up on life.
If you give up that first time, it's easier to give up the second,
third, and fourth times.

Tom Watson

❧

Confidence builds with successive putts.
The putter, then, is a club designed to hit the ball partway to the hole.

Rex Lardner

Most golfers prepare for disaster.
A good golfer prepares for success.
Bob Toski

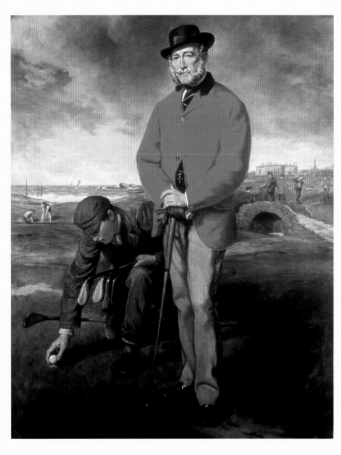

The Golfer's Book of Quotations

If a ball comes to rest in dangerous proximity to a hippopotamus
or crocodile, another ball may be dropped at a safe distance,
no nearer the hole, without penalty.

Local Rule: Nyanza Club, British East Africa in the 1950s

❦

I call my putter 'Sweet Charity' because it covers such a multitude
of sins from tee to green.

Billy Casper

❦

Real golfers don't cry when they line up their fourth putt.

Karen Hurwitz

The Golfer's Book of Quotations

Players should pick up bomb and shell splinters from the fairways
in order to save damage to the mowers.

British War Rule

Over the years, I've studied habits of golfers. I know what to look for.
Watch their eyes. Fear shows up when there is an enlargement of the pupils.
Big pupils lead to big scores.

Sam Snead

The person I fear most in the last two rounds is myself.

Tom Watson (at the US Open)

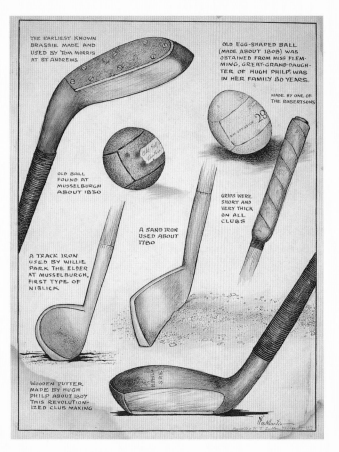

THE EARLIEST KNOWN BRASSIE MADE AND USED BY TOM MORRIS AT ST ANDREWS

OLD EGG-SHAPED BALL (MADE ABOUT 1808) WAS OBTAINED FROM MISS FLEMMING, GREAT-GRAND-DAUGHTER OF HUGH PHILP. WAS IN HER FAMILY 80 YEARS.

MADE BY ONE OF THE ROBERTSONS

OLD BALL FOUND AT MUSSELBURGH ABOUT 1830

GRIPS WERE SHORT AND VERY THICK ON ALL CLUBS

A SAND IRON USED ABOUT 1780

A TRACK IRON USED BY WILLIE PARK THE ELDER AT MUSSELBURGH, FIRST TYPE OF NIBLICK

WOODEN PUTTER MADE BY HUGH PHILP ABOUT 1807 THIS REVOLUTIONIZED CLUB MAKING

Golf is a game whose aim is to hit a very small ball into an even smaller hole, with weapons singularly ill-designed for the purpose.

Sir Winston Churchill

The Golfer's Book of Quotations

The nice thing about these [golf] books is that they usually cancel each other out. One book tells you to keep your eye on the ball; the next says not to bother. Personally, in the crowd I play with, a better idea is to keep your eye on your partner.

Jim Murray

※

You've just one problem. You stand too close to the ball – after you've hit it.

Sam Snead (to a pupil)

※

At least he can't cheat on his score – because all you have to do is look back down the fairway and count the wounded.

Bob Hope

The Golfer's Book of Quotations

He enjoys that perfect peace, that peace beyond all understanding,
which comes at its maximum only to the man who has given up golf.

P G Wodehouse

Sure, the purses are obscene.
The average worker, let's say, makes $25,000 a year, while a golfer makes
$25,000 for finishing 10th. Our values have departed somewhat.

Tom Watson (1989)

Always throw clubs ahead of you.
That way you don't have to waste energy going back to pick them up.

Tommy Bolt

The Golfer's Book of Quotations

The average expert player – if he is lucky – hits six, eight or ten real shots in a round. The rest are good misses.

Tommy Armour

True golfers do not play the game as a form of stress management. Quite the reverse. They play to establish superiority over (a) themselves, (b) inanimate objects such as a small white ball with dimples in it, and (c) their friends. All of which can become rather tedious.

Colin Bowles

Everyone gets wounded in a game of golf. The trick is not to bleed.

Peter Dobereiner

The Golfer's Book of Quotations

Play is conducted at a snail's pace.
Some golfers today remind me of kids walking to school and praying
they'll be late. . . . Golfers used to check the grass of the greens;
today they study the roots under each blade.

Jimmy Demaret (1954)

I've noticed some of them are off balance when they swing.
They're top-heavy. They've got too much hair.

Ben Hogan on today's golfers (1970)

Stroke play is a better test of golf, but match play is a better test of character.

Joe Carr

The Golfer's Book of Quotations

I was afraid to move my lips in front of TV. The Commissioner probably
would have fined me just for what I was thinking.

Tom Weiskopf (on his 13 in the 1980 Masters)

❦

It is nothing new or original to say that golf is played one stroke at a time.
But it took me many years to realise it.

Bobby Jones

❦

If you try to break the ball to pieces,
the sod may fly farther than your shots. You've got to be gentle.
Sweet-talk that ball. Make it your friend and it will stay with you a lot longer.

Sam Snead

The Golfer's Book of Quotations

I always keep a supply of stimulants handy in case I see a snake,
which I also keep handy.

W C Fields (putting whisky in his golf bag)

Golf acts as a corrective against sinful pride. I attribute the insane
arrogance of the later Roman emperors almost entirely to the fact that,
never having played golf, they never knew that strange chastening humility
which is engendered by a topped chip shot.

P G Wodehouse

If you keep shooting par at them, they all crack up sooner or later.

Bobby Jones

The Golfer's Book of Quotations

What the nineteenth hole proves beyond a shadow of a doubt
is that the Scots invented the game solely in order to sell their
national beverage in large quantities.

Milton Gross

A good player who is a great putter is a match for any golfer.
A great hitter who cannot putt is a match for no one.

Ben Sayers

Fairway: A narrow strip of mown grass that separates two groups of golfers
looking for lost balls in the rough.

Henry Beard & Roy McKie

The Golfer's Book of Quotations

A secret disbelief in the enemy's play is very useful for match play.

Sir Walter Simpson

No matter what happens – never give up a hole. . . .
In tossing in your cards after a bad beginning you also undermine your whole game, because to quit between tee and green is more habit-forming than drinking a highball before breakfast.

Sam Snead

Water creates a neurosis in golfers. The very thought of this harmless fluid robs them of their normal powers of rational thought, turns their legs to jelly, and produces a palsy of the upper limbs.

Peter Dobereiner

CADDIE (*as famous surgeon misses another short putt*). "Lummy! fancy bein' operated on by 'im!"

No man has mastered golf until he has realised that his good shots are accidents and his bad shots good exercise.

Eugene R Black

The Golfer's Book of Quotations

If the tree is skinny, aim right at it.
A peculiarity of golf is that what you aim at you generally miss, . . .
the success of the shot depending mainly, of course,
on your definition of 'skinny.'

Rex Lardner

❦

President Ford waits until he hits his first drive to know
what course he's playing that day.

Bob Hope

❦

When they start hitting back at me, it's time to quit.

Henry Ransom (when a shot rebounded from a cliff and hit him in the stomach)

The Golfer's Book of Quotations

Arnold Palmer had everything except a brake pedal.

Peter Dobereiner

❧

The fundamental problem with golf is that every so often, no matter how lacking you may be in the essential virtues required of a steady player, the odds are that one day you will hit the ball straight, hard and out of sight.
This is the essential frustration of this excruciating sport. For when you've done it once, you make the fundamental error of asking yourself why you can't do it all the time. The answer to this question is simple: the first time was a fluke.

Colin Bowles

❧

He hits it in the woods so often he should get an orange hunting jacket.

Tom Weiskopf on Ben Crenshaw

The Golfer's Book of Quotations

The difference between golf and government is that in golf
you can't improve your lie.

George Deukmejian (Governor of California)

❧

You get to know more of the character of a man in a round of golf than
you can get to know in six months with only political experience.

David Lloyd George

❧

The golfer has more enemies than any other athlete. He has 14 clubs in his
bag, all of them different; 18 holes to play, all of them different, every week;
and all around him are sand, trees, grass, water, wind and 143 other players.
In addition, the game is fifty percent mental, so his biggest enemy is himself.

Dan Jenkins

The Golfer's Book of Quotations

I'm only scared of three things – lightning, a side-hill putt,
and Ben Hogan.

Sam Snead

❦

The only difference between an amateur and a pro is that we call a shot that
goes left-to-right a fade and an amateur calls it a slice.

Peter Jacobsen

❦

Playing against him [Gary Player],
you begin hoping he'll be on grass rather than in sand. From grass you expect
him to pitch the ball close. From a bunker you're afraid he'll hole it out!

Jack Nicklaus

Golf is like art;
it's impossible to be perfect.

Sandra Palmer

The Golfer's Book of Quotations

Pressure is going out there on the golf course and thinking,
'If I don't do well, I'll have to rob another bank.'

Rick Meissner (former touring pro & convicted bank robber)

❧

I said to the writers, 'There's Nicklaus, for example, only five strokes back.
I wouldn't feel safe from Jack if he was in a wheelchair.'

Dan Jenkins

❧

[Tom] Watson scares me. If he's lying six in the middle of the fairway,
there's some kind of way he might make a five.

Lee Trevino

The Golfer's Book of Quotations

If profanity had an influence on the flight of the ball,
the game would be played far better than it is.

Horace G Hutchinson

⁂

Hole-in-One: An occurrence in which a ball is hit directly from the tee
into the hole on a single shot by a golfer playing alone.

Henry Beard & Roy McKie

⁂

I know I'm getting better at golf
because I'm hitting fewer spectators.

Gerald Ford

The Golfer's Book of Quotations

He goes after a golf course like a lion at a zebra.
He doesn't reason with it; he tries to throw it out of the window
or hold its head under water till it stops wriggling.

Jim Murray on Seve Ballesteros

❧

The player may experiment about his swing, his grip, his stance.
It is only when he begins asking his caddie's advice that he is
getting on dangerous ground.

Sir Walter Simpson

❧

Winning isn't everything, but wanting to win is.

Arnold Palmer

The Golfer's Book of Quotations

In the actual playing of the game, the golfer cannot keep a great amount of theory in mind and have any attention left to bestow upon the ball.

John Dunn

If your adversary is a hole or two down, there is no serious cause for alarm in his complaining of a severely sprained wrist. . . . Should he happen to win the next hole, these symptoms will in all probability become less troublesome.

Horace G Hutchinson

What is love compared with holing out before your opponent?

P G Wodehouse

The Golfer's Book of Quotations

It is ridiculous to suggest, as some people do, that golf is a dangerous game.
I myself have only been struck three times this season!

W T Linskill

It is better to smash your clubs than to lose your temper.

Lord Balfour

Golf is like art;
There are three ways of learning golf:
by study, which is the most wearisome; by imitation, which is the most
fallacious; and by experience, which is the most bitter.

Robert Browning

The Golfer's Book of Quotations

Golf is so popular simply because it is the best game in the world at which to be bad. . . . At golf it is the bad player who gets the most strokes.

A A Milne

❧⚜❧

I am quite certain that there has never been a greater addition to the lighter side of civilization than that supplied by the game of golf.

Lord Balfour

❧⚜❧

Golfers find it a very trying matter to turn at the waist, more particularly if they have a lot of waist to turn.

Harry Vardon

The Golfer's Book of Quotations

It's good sportsmanship to not pick up lost golf balls while they are still rolling.

Mark Twain

The trouble with this game is that they say the good breaks and bad breaks
even up. What they don't tell you is that they don't even up right away.
You might go two or three years and all you get is bad-break
bad-break bad-break.
That gets annoying in a hurry.

Johnny Miller

Nobody ever swung the golf club too slowly.

Bobby Jones

The Golfer's Book of Quotations

A Scotsman is the only golfer not trying to hit the ball out of sight.

Anon

❧

The amateur who picks up his newspaper and remarks that he could shoot better golf than those guys on tour should pause and consider the prospects very carefully . . . It is not just a different game. It is not a game at all.

Peter Dobereiner

❧

Golf may be . . . a sophisticated game. At least, it is usually played with the outward appearance of great dignity. It is, nevertheless, a game of considerable passion, either of the explosive type, or that which burns inwardly and sears the soul.

Bobby Jones

The little white ball won't move until you've hit it, and there's nothing you can do after it has gone.

Babe Didrikson Zaharias

HEART-BROKEN COMPETITOR (*who has missed a quick putt*). "Now wouldn't you call that provoking?"
CADDIE. "Well, Miss, that's a word I don't use meself."

The Golfer's Book of Quotations

If you don't succeed at first, don't despair. Remember it takes time
to learn to play golf; most players spend their entire lifetime finding
out about the game before they give it up.

Stephen Baker

The wit of man has never invented a pastime equal to golf for
its healthful recreation, its pleasurable excitement, and its never ending
source of amusement.

Lord Balfour

Golf is an indispensable adjunct to high civilisation.

Andrew Carnegie

The Golfer's Book of Quotations

It is a strange thing that we know just how to do a thing at golf,
and yet we cannot do it.

Bernard Darwin

Golf is the only game where the worst player gets the best of it. He obtains
more out of it as regards both exercise and enjoyment, for the good player gets
worried over the slightest mistake, whereas the poor player makes too many
mistakes to worry over them.

David Lloyd George

A golf game doesn't end until the last putt drops.

Cary Middlecoff

Acknowledgements:

'Copies Golfers', Edwardian Cigarette Cards in an Album
Private Collection/Bridgeman Art Library, London

Portrait of John Whyte Melville of Bennochy and Strathkinness,
Captain of the Club 1823 by Sir Francis Grant (1810-1878)
Royal & Ancient Golf Club, St Andrews/Bridgeman Art Library, London

Ladies Match at Westward Ho! by Francis Powell Hopkins (1830-1913)
Private Collection/Bridgeman Art Library, London

Golfing at Westward Ho! by Francis Powell Hopkins (1830-1913)
Private Collection/Bridgeman Art Library, London

Oil Study for Frontispiece of R Clark's 'Golf - A Royal & Ancient Game.' by Clark Stanton (1823-1894)
Private Collection/Bridgeman Art Library, London

View of Military Players at St Andrews, late 17th century English School (17th century),
Royal & Ancient Golf Club, St Andrews
© Phaidon Press Ltd/David Cripps/Brigeman Art Library, London

Other illustrations © Robert Frederick Archives